DATE DUE

A PRIMARY SOURCE HISTORY
OF THE UNITED STATES

AMERICA AND
THE COLD WAR

1949–1969

George E. Stanley

WORLD ALMANAC® LIBRARY

Please visit our web site at: www.worldalmanaclibrary.com
For a free color catalog describing World Almanac® Library's list of high-quality
books and multimedia programs, call 1-800-848-2928 (USA) or 1-800-387-3178
(Canada). World Almanac® Library's fax: (414) 332-3567.

Library of Congress Cataloging-in-Publication Data available upon request from publisher.
Fax (414) 336-0157 for the attention of the Publishing Records Department.

ISBN 0-8368-5830-1 (lib. bdg.)
ISBN 0-8368-5839-5 (softcover)

First published in 2005 by
World Almanac® Library
330 West Olive Street, Suite 100
Milwaukee, WI 53212 USA

Produced by Byron Preiss Visual Publications Inc.
Project Editor: Susan Hoe
Designer: Marisa Gentile
World Almanac® Library editor: Alan Wachtel
World Almanac® Library art direction: Tammy West

Picture acknowledgements:
AP/Wide World Photos: Cover (lower left, upper right, lower right), p. 9. CORBIS: p. 24.
HistoryPictures.com: p. 25. Library of Congress: Cover (upper left), pp. 5, 6, 7, 10, 13, 15,
16, 18, 21, 22, 23, 27, 28, 30, 31, 32, 33, 35, 37, 38, 39. NASA: p. 43. National Archives
and Records Administration: p. 40.

Printed in the United States of America

1 2 3 4 5 6 7 8 9 09 08 07 06 05

Dr. George E. Stanley is a professor at Cameron University in Lawton, Oklahoma. He has authored
more than eighty books for young readers, many in the field of history and science. Dr. Stanley recently
completed a series of history books on famous Americans, including *Geronimo, Andrew Jackson,
Harry S. Truman*, and *Mr. Rogers*.

CONTENTS

Through the examination of authentic historical documents, including charters, diaries, journals, letters, speeches, and other written records, each title in *A Primary Source History of the United States* offers a unique perspective on the events that shaped the United States. In addition to providing important historical information, each document serves as a piece of living history that opens a window into the kinds of thinking and modes of expression that characterized the various epochs of American history.

Note: To facilitate the reading of older documents, the modern-day spelling of certain words is used.

CHAPTER 1

The End of the Truman Years

1949–1953

At the end of World War II, Americans were ready to enjoy the fruits of peace after years of depression and wartime sacrifice, but tensions with the Soviet Union— the leader of the Communist world — created political and economic conflicts, which became known as the "Cold War." To combat these threats, the United States formed new alliances and provided economic and military aid to weakened democracies. The onset of the Cold War also affected domestic politics. Fear of internal subversion led to congressional investigations of Communist infiltration of the movie industry, the government, and even the United States Army.

After World War II, the Korean Peninsula was occupied by the Soviet Union and the United States, but President Truman soon realized that in order to keep the Soviets from trying to occupy the entire peninsula, Korea should be divided at the thirty-eighth parallel—the middle of the country. Joseph Stalin, the leader of the Soviet Union, agreed—the United States would control the south and the Soviet Union, the north.

Over the next five years, the United States and the Soviet Union could not reach a decision on how best to prepare a united Korea for full independence, and in 1948, Korea was split into two separate countries—the People's Democratic Republic of Korea, which had a Communist-led government, and the Republic of Korea, which was supported by the United States.

THE KOREAN WAR

On June 25, 1950, the North Korean army invaded South Korea. President Truman, a driving force behind the creation of the United Nations—an organization that was formed in 1945 to bring the nations of the world together to discuss how best to solve their problems peacefully—immediately took the matter to the United Nations Security Council.

The United Nations Security

The Security Council, having determined that the armed attack upon the Republic of Korea by forces from North Korea constitutes a breach of the peace, having called for an immediate cessation of hostilities, and having called upon the authorities of North Korea to withdraw forthwith their armed forces to the 38th parallel, and having noted ... that the authorities in North Korea have neither ceased hostilities nor withdrawn their armed forces to the 38th parallel and that urgent military measures are required to restore international peace and security ... recommends that the Members of the United Nations furnish such assistance to the Republic of Korea as may be necessary to repel the armed attack and to restore international peace and security in the area.

Council adopted a resolution declaring North Korea to be the aggressor and recommending that member nations render aid under its auspices to South Korea. Because the Soviet Union's representative was not present at the meeting to exercise his country's veto, the resolution was passed. Although the United Nations forces consisted of units from seventeen countries, the bulk of the combat forces came from the United States and South Korea.

In the early months of the war, the North Koreans were successful, because the invasion had taken the South

Koreans by surprise, but in the fall of 1950, American troops, under the command of General Douglas MacArthur, landed at the western port

▲ Driving past cheering Koreans, U.S. troops make their way to the thirty-eighth parallel in 1950.

city of Inchon, decisively cutting the already tenuous North Korean supply lines. They captured the nearby capital of Seoul and moved across the thirty-eighth parallel deep into North Korea.

In November 1950, the new Communist government of China sent its troops across its border with North Korea. It was determined to drive the United Nations forces from the entire Korean peninsula. The United Nations General Assembly condemned China's action. General MacArthur wanted to launch a counteroffensive by attacking China, but President Truman believed that such an invasion would force the Soviet

▲ General Douglas MacArthur and other army officers at the front line in Korea.

TRUMAN'S BROADCAST ADDRESS: APRIL 11, 1951

I want to talk plainly to you tonight about what we are doing in Korea.... We are trying to prevent a third world war....

I believe that we must try to limit war to Korea [instead of expanding it into China]....

A number of events have made it evident that General MacArthur did not agree with that policy. I have therefore considered it essential to relieve General MacArthur [of his command] so that there would be no doubt or confusion as to the real purpose and aim of our policy.

It was with the deepest personal regret that I found myself compelled to take this action. General MacArthur is one of our greatest military commanders. But the cause of world peace is more important than any individual....

We are ready, at any time, to negotiate for a restoration of peace in the area. But we will not engage in appeasement. We are only interested in real peace....

Union and Communist China to declare war on the United States, something he didn't want, so he vetoed the plan.

When MacArthur complained in public about Truman's decision, the president relieved him of his command. Although some people hailed MacArthur as a hero, most Americans agreed that the president's action was needed to keep the fighting from developing into World War III.

In June 1951, the Soviet Union suggested holding cease-fire talks. Negotiations dragged on for months. Armistice talks began in July 1951, but the fighting and dying went on for two more years. An armistice was finally signed in July 1953, fixing the thirty-eighth parallel as the border between North and South Korea.

McCarthyism

When the Soviet Union exploded its atomic bomb in 1949—long before anyone expected it—there was public suspicion that some Americans were actively working to help the Communist cause. A period of anti-Communist hysteria—known as McCarthyism—was driven by a Republican senator from Wisconsin named Joseph McCarthy. He used "Communists in government" as an

▲ **A portrait of Senator Joseph McCarthy taken in 1954.**

issue to help get himself elected to a second term in 1952. That year, Republicans gained control of Congress, and McCarthy became even more powerful, continuing his search for subversives.

He questioned the loyalty of Secretary of State Dean Acheson and Secretary of Defense George Marshall. During the Army-McCarthy hearings, which were televised nationally between April and June 1954, McCarthy accused the army of being "soft" on Communism. He came across as a bully and a demagogue.

In a 1950 speech to a West Virginia women's club, McCarthy spoke of the "enemies within" and pointed to the State Department.

McCARTHY'S SPEECH TO A WOMEN'S CLUB: 1950

... As one of our outstanding historical figures once said, "When a great democracy is destroyed, it will not be because of enemies from without, but rather because of enemies from within."

The reason we find ourselves in a position of impotency is not because our only powerful potential enemy has sent men to invade our shores, but rather because of the traitorous actions of those who have been treated so well by this Nation. It has not been the less fortunate or members of minority groups who have been selling this nation out, but rather those who have had all the benefits that the wealthiest nation on earth has to offer....

This is glaringly true in the State Department.... In my opinion, the State Department, which is one of the most important government departments, is thoroughly infested with Communists....

Margaret Chase Smith of Maine, the first woman to be elected to the U.S. Senate, was known as the conscience of the Senate. She had a reputation for courage and independence. In her "Declaration of Conscience" speech, on June 1, 1950, she denounced the tactics used by Senator McCarthy in his anti-Communist crusade. Senator Chase stated, "The American people are sick and tired of being afraid to speak their minds lest they be politically smeared as 'Communists' or 'Fascists' by their opponents. Freedom of speech is not what it used to be in America. It has been so abused by some that it is not exercised by others...."

Senator Smith never mentioned Senator McCarthy by name, but there was no doubt about whom she was talking. McCarthy threatened to ruin Smith's career, but his tactics failed. Smith was so highly regarded in Maine that she was easily reelected in 1954. Senator McCarthy, on the other hand, was censured (given an official disapproval) by the Senate in December 1954 and died a broken man three years later.

TRUMAN'S TERM COMES TO AN END

As president of the United States, Harry S. Truman was the leader of what was known at the time as the

TRUMAN'S LETTER TO PAUL HUME: 1950

Mr. Hume:

I've just read your lousy review of Margaret's concert. I've come to the conclusion that you are an "eight ulcer man on four ulcer pay."

It seems to me that you are a frustrated old man who wishes he could have been successful. When you write such poppy-cock as was in the back section of the paper you work for it shows conclusively that you're off the beam and at least four of your ulcers are at work.

Some day I hope to meet you. When that happens you'll need a new nose, a lot of beefsteak for black eyes, and perhaps a supporter below!...

"Free World." He was also a devoted and protective family man. On December 5, 1950, his daughter, Margaret, an aspiring opera singer, gave a concert at Constitution Hall in Washington, D.C. When Truman picked up his *Washington Post* the next morning to read a review of his daughter's singing performance, he became livid. Though conceding that Miss Truman was "extremely attractive," Paul Hume, the *Post's* music critic, stated bluntly that "Miss Truman cannot sing very well" and "has not improved" over the years. The president wrote a letter to Hume in which he used language that many people thought was "unpresidential," but it was right in character with Truman's no-nonsense Midwestern personality.

In 1952, when President Truman decided not to run for reelection because he had lost the New Hampshire Democratic presidential primary to Senator Estes Kefauver of Tennessee, the Democratic nomination opened up, and Governor Adlai Stevenson of Illinois became the party's candidate.

▲ President Truman *(left)* and presidential nominee Adlai Stevenson at the 1952 Democratic convention.

CHAPTER 2

The Eisenhower Years

1953–1960

During the 1952 election, the Republicans nominated General Dwight D. Eisenhower, a hero of World War II. For some Republicans, Eisenhower was too soft on Communism, so Richard Nixon was named his vice-presidential running mate to placate the anti-Communist wing of the party.

Nixon, a congressman from California, was—along with Senator Joseph McCarthy—a high-profile member of the House Committee on Un-American Activities, which investigated citizens who were accused of being disloyal

▲ Vice president elect and Mrs. Nixon celebrate after winning the 1952 election.

and of belonging to subversive organizations. Riding this wave of anti-Communist hysteria, Nixon was elected to the U.S. Senate in 1950.

NIXON'S "CHECKERS" SPEECH: 1952

... Not one cent of the $18,000 or any other money of that type ever went to me for my personal use. Every penny of it was used to pay for political expenses that I did not think should be charged to the taxpayers of the United States....

One other thing I probably should tell you because if we don't they'll probably be saying this about me too, we did get something—a gift—after the election.... It was a little cocker spaniel dog in a crate that [a man had] sent all the way from Texas. Black and white spotted. And our little girl—Tricia, the 6-year old—named it Checkers. And you know ... regardless of what they say about it, we're gonna keep it....

During the campaign, the *New York Post* accused Nixon of using some of his campaign money for personal instead of political expenses. Several senior advisers to presidential candidate Dwight D. Eisenhower told him he should drop Nixon from the ticket. Nixon went on national television and explained the situation in what was called the "Checkers Speech," because of a reference to a puppy, which a supporter in Texas had given his daughter—and which Nixon said he was not going to return. The speech kept Nixon on the Republican ticket, and Eisenhower, because of his enormous popularity, handily defeated Stevenson.

During the 1952 presidential campaign, Eisenhower pledged to end the war in Korea. He kept his promise. When the armistice was finally signed on July 27—after each side agreed on how prionsers of war would be released—President Eisenhower went on the air to announce the long sought-after end to the fighting.

EISENHOWER'S ADDRESS TO THE NATION: 1953

... My Fellow Citizens: Tonight we greet, with prayers of thanksgiving, the official news that an armistice was signed almost an hour ago in Korea. It will quickly bring to an end the fighting between the United Nations forces and the Communist armies. And so at long last the carnage of war is to cease.... For this nation the cost of repelling aggression has been high. In thousands of homes it has been incalculable.... We and our United Nations allies must be vigilant against the possibility of untoward developments.

And, as we do so, we shall fervently strive to insure that this armistice will, in fact, bring free peoples one step nearer to a goal of a world of peace....

EISENHOWER AND VIETNAM

The Geneva Peace Accords, signed by France and Vietnam in 1954, marked the end of French control of Indochina. Pressure from the Soviet Union and Communist China forced the Vietnamese to agree to a temporary partition of their country at the seventeenth parallel, but the United States thought the accords gave too much power to Vietnam's Communist Party.

In a letter to South Vietnamese president Ngo Dinh Diem, President Eisenhower promised him support to resist any Communist subversion or aggression, but Eisenhower stressed that Diem's government also needed to improve the living standards of its citizens. This constituted one of the first steps in America's eventual involvement in the Vietnam War.

EISENHOWER'S LETTER TO NGO DINH DIEM: 1954

… I am … instructing the American Ambassador to Vietnam to examine with you … how an intelligent program of American aid given directly to your Government can … assist Vietnam in its present hour of trial, provided that your Government is prepared to give assurances as to the standards of performance it would be able to maintain in the event such aid were supplied.…

THE ROSENBERG TRIAL

Americans firmly believed that Communists not only wanted to take over the rest of the world but also planned to destroy the United States—possibly with atomic bombs. Shelters sprang up everywhere, and almost daily, school children practiced what they would need to do if an attack came.

In the spring of 1950, evidence emerged about David Greenglass, an army sergeant who was stationed during the war at the secret Manhattan Project laboratory in Los Alamos, New Mexico, where the atomic bomb had been built, that he had provided information about nuclear research to Soviet agents. He claimed that he had been recruited by Ethel and Julius Rosenberg, his sister and brother-in-law.

That summer, FBI agents arrested

the Rosenbergs for espionage. Although the couple insisted they were innocent, they were tried, convicted, and sentenced to die in the electric chair. National and international protests followed, but the Supreme Court voted six to three in favor of their execution.

Clyde Miller, a former colleague of President Eisenhower, wrote him a letter, asking Eisenhower to grant the Rosenbergs clemency—that is, overturn the death sentence. In July 1953, Eisenhower explained why he could not do that.

▲ The Rosenbergs after being being found guilty of espionage in 1951.

EISENHOWER'S LETTER TO CLYDE MILLER: 1953

June 10, 1953

Dear Clyde:

Thank you very much for your thoughts on the Rosenberg conviction....

The action of these people [the Rosenbergs] has exposed to great danger of death literally millions of our citizens. The very real question becomes how far can this be permitted by a government that, regardless of every consideration of mercy and compassion, is also required to be a just government in serving the interests of all its citizens....

When it comes to the decision to commute such a sentence—which would mean that these arch criminals would be subject to parole at the end of fifteen years—I must say I have not yet been able to justify such an action....

I know that you wrote out of a deep sense of duty and friendship ... but I doubt that you have had to consider some of the results that could spring from the action you recommend....

On June 19, 1953, the Rosenbergs wrote a final letter to their two sons, Michael, ten, and Robert, six. Later that same day, Julius and Ethel were electrocuted, the first U.S. civilians to be put to death for espionage. In late 2001, Greenglass, who only served ten years in prison, admitted that he had lied at the trial about his sister's involvement in the spy case in order to protect his wife and children. Although there is strong evidence that Julius was guilty, the Rosenbergs professed their innocence to their sons.

THE ROSENBERGS' LETTER TO THEIR CHILDREN: 1953

> **Your lives must teach you, too, that good cannot really flourish in the midst of evil.**

Dearest Sweethearts, my most precious children,

Only this morning it looked like we might be together again after all. Now that this cannot be I want so much for you to know all that I have come to know. Unfortunately I may write only a few simple words....

At first, of course, you will grieve bitterly for us, but you will not grieve alone. This is our consolation and it must eventually be yours.

Eventually, too, you must come to believe that life is worth the living. Be comforted that even now, with the end of ours slowly approaching that we know this with a conviction that defeats the executioner!

Your lives must teach you, too, that good cannot really flourish in the midst of evil; that freedom and all the things that go to make up a truly satisfying and worthwhile life, must sometimes be purchased very dearly. Be comforted, then, that we were serene and understood with the deepest kind of understanding, that civilization had not as yet progressed to the point where life did not have to be lost for the sake of life....

We wish we might have had the tremendous joy and

gratification of living our lives out with you. Your Daddy who is with me in these last momentous hours sends his heart and all the love that is in it for his dearest boys. Always remember that we were innocent and could not wrong our conscience.

We press you close and kiss you with all our strength.

Lovingly,

Daddy and Mommy

PROSPERITY DURING THE 1950S

The 1950s were seen as a period of prosperity and, after the Korean War ended, peace. Middle-class Americans had more money to spend, and they spent it on cars, homes, and television sets. The influx of people to the suburbs continued throughout the decade. The growth of these "bedroom communities," where residents lived on the outskirts of a city and commuted to work, meant that the automobile was no longer considered a luxury. As the number of cars increased, so did the demand for gasoline and better roads. The "American dream" of owning your own home became a reality for many Americans. An ad in the June 25, 1950, edition of the *New York Times* carried a message directed at potential home buyers in the New York City suburbs.

◀ A typical house in the Levittown development in 1958.

ADVERTISEMENT FOR A HOME: 1950

Six rooms, all on one floor, attached garage, full basement, 34 by 25, exclusive of laundry space, make this a complete home for all the family—comfortable to live in, easy to keep, interesting and inviting to your friends....

The basement easily becomes a recreation or hobby room, a play place for the children....

The ... all-electric kitchen lightens housework.... Refrigerator, range, dishwasher, ventilating fan and washing machine (in the basement) all are included in the purchase price ... [of] $14,790 for everything mentioned, plus ... 6,000-square foot landscaped plot, sewers, curb, paved street, sidewalk. Veterans pay nothing down. Their 30-year mortgages bear 4 percent interest. Terms to non-veterans are equally attractive....

17 miles from midtown [Manhattan] or Brooklyn....

THE END OF POLIO

For the most part, the physical well-being of Americans was as good as their economic health, but some medical scientists, such as Dr. Jonas Salk, hoped to make it even better.

In 1947, Salk became the head of the Virus Research Lab at the University of Pittsburgh. He worked on improving the flu vaccine and began to study the polio virus—a disease that caused muscle paralysis in humans and could even result in death. He hoped to create a vaccine for the polio virus as well.

Since the turn of the century, polio outbreaks had grown more

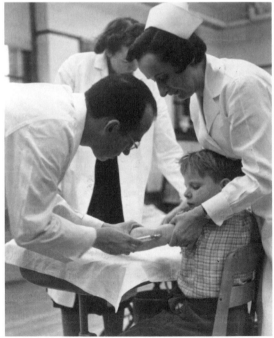

▲ Dr. Jonas Salk inoculates a little boy with his polio vaccine in the 1950s.

SALK'S LETTER TO MRS. ROOSEVELT: 1955

March 26, 1955

Dear Mrs. Roosevelt:

A desire I have had for a long time has overtaken me. I suppose this has occurred because the time is drawing quite near when a report will be made which, I expect, will indicate that a means for preventing paralytic poliomyelitis is available. Since you were the person closest to the man to whom society owes so great a debt, I wanted you to know that my thoughts, in the past few years, have been with you and your late husband more often than I can count.

The scientific report, that may mark the beginning of the end of the scourge of polio, is to be made on the Tenth Anniversary of Mr. Roosevelt's untimely death. Wherever you may be, or whatever your thoughts, I would like you to know that a part of his great spirit will be within me, living as it was during his great life, while we all share the knowledge that may bring the fulfillment of the dream he had many years ago....

> **"**The scientific report, that may mark the beginning of the end of the scourge of polio, is to be made.**"**

frequent and more devastating. In 1952, some estimates recorded 57,628 cases, making it the worst year yet.

In 1952, Dr. Salk came up with a new vaccine that he believed was safe and effective. He inoculated volunteers, including himself, his wife, and their three sons, with his experimental polio vaccine. Everyone who received the test vaccine began producing specific antibodies that would protect them against the disease, and no one became ill. Nationwide testing was soon carried out.

Right before the successful results were to be announced to the public, Dr. Salk wrote a letter to Eleanor Roosevelt, the widow of the nation's most famous polio victim, President Franklin D. Roosevelt.

By developing a successful vaccine at the peak of polio's devastation, Dr. Salk won instant fame.

EISENHOWER'S ECONOMIC POLICIES

During the 1950s, President Eisenhower expanded on some of Franklin Roosevelt's programs. Social Security now covered the self-employed, farm workers, and military personnel, and the federal minimum wage rose to $1 an hour. During his administration, Eisenhower cut farm subsidies and promoted private rather than public development of the national energy resources.

Even though Eisenhower was committed to limiting the role that the federal government played in the economy, he used the power and the resources of the federal government during his administration to start two major public works projects—the St. Lawrence Seaway and the interstate highway system.

The Seaway, completed in 1959, was a joint American-Canadian effort. Ocean-going ships now had access to the ports of the Great Lakes. Eisenhower believed the nation's highway system was inadequate in case of an attack on key cities. The Interstate Highway Act, passed in 1956, authorized the government to pay for ninety percent of the cost of building the highway system through a tax on automobiles and gasoline. Since this thirty-year construction program favored cars and trucks, spending on urban mass transit and railroads was reduced.

▲ After the Interstate Highway Act of 1956, more interstate highways were built.

CIVIL RIGHTS IN THE 1950s

During the Eisenhower administration, Congress did very little to improve the legal status of blacks and other minorities.

In 1950, the National Association for the Advancement of Colored People (NAACP) Legal Defense and Education Fund decided to challenge the legality of the 1896 Supreme Court decision *Plessy* v. *Ferguson*, which established the "separate but equal" doctrine. At the same time, several other challenges—all supported by the NAACP—were making their way through the court system. One of the first to reach the Supreme Court was *Brown* v. *Board of Education of Topeka, Kansas,* in 1954. The Court, under the newly appointed chief justice Earl Warren, ruled that "separate but equal" schools for white and blacks were separate but were not really equal and were, therefore, a violation of the equal protection

BROWN V. BOARD OF EDUCATION OF TOPEKA, KANSAS: 1954

... In approaching this problem, we cannot turn the clock back to ... 1896 when Plessy v. Ferguson [separate but equal ruling] was written. We must consider public education in the light of its full development and its present place in American life throughout the Nation. Only in this way can it be determined if segregation in public schools deprives these plaintiffs of the equal protection of the laws....

We believe it does....

We conclude that in the field of public education the doctrine of "separate but equal" has no place. Separate education facilities are inherently unequal. Therefore, we hold that the plaintiffs and others similarly situated for whom the actions have been brought are, by reason of the segregation complained of, deprived of the equal protection of the laws guaranteed by the Fourteenth Amendment....

clause of the Fourteenth Amendment to the U.S. Constitution. Warren knew that for the Court's decision to have a significant impact across the country, it had to be unanimous, so he worked hard to make sure that it was. Although the Court did not provide a blueprint as to how its decision should be carried out, in 1955, it ordered the desegregation of all public schools "with all deliberate speed."

Following the decision, President Eisenhower ordered the immediate desegregation of the schools in Washington, D.C. The process went smoothly there, as well as in most of the other twenty-one states that still had legally segregated school systems. In some states, however, especially in the South, opposition to integration was strong. People who vehemently opposed integration revived the Ku Klux Klan and created White Citizens' Councils whose sole purpose was to defend segregation.

ROSA PARKS

In the 1950s, laws in Montgomery, Alabama, still required blacks to sit in the back of public busses, while whites sat in the front. The imaginary line that separated the races would gradually move toward the back, as more whites got on. No white person ever stood while a black person sat, but it wasn't unusual for blacks to stand, even if the white section wasn't full.

On Thursday night, December 1, 1955, after an exhausting day of work at a downtown Montgomery department store, forty-two-year-old seamstress Rosa Parks boarded a city bus for the trip home and sat in the first row reserved for blacks. Soon all of the white seats were filled. At the next stop, when other white people got on, the bus driver ordered Mrs. Parks and three other black people to leave their row and stand at the back of the bus. The other people complied, but Mrs. Parks refused. The bus driver called the police, and Mrs. Parks was arrested.

When E. D. Nixon, a former head of the local NAACP, heard what had happened, he raised money for Mrs. Parks's bail. Although Rosa Parks was not the first black person to refuse to give up a seat on a Montgomery bus, her defiant action started a movement against legal segregation and precipitated the Montgomery Bus Boycott.

In an interview on the Scholastic Books Web site in 1997, Mrs. Parks gave her version of what happened on the bus that day in 1955.

AN INTERVIEW WITH ROSA PARKS: 1997

… I did not sit at the very front of the bus. I took a seat with a man who was next to the window—the first seat that was allowed for "colored" people to sit in. We were not disturbed until we reached the third stop after I boarded the bus. At this point, a few white people boarded the bus, and one white man was left standing. When the driver noticed him, he told us [the blacks] to let the man have the seat. The other [blacks] all stood up. But the driver saw me still sitting there. He said I should stand up, and I said, "No, I will not." Then he said, "I'll have you arrested." And I told him he could do that. So he didn't move the bus any further. Several [black] people left the bus. Two policemen got on the bus in a couple of minutes. The driver told the police that I would not stand up. [One] policeman walked down [the aisle] and asked me why I didn't stand up, and I said I didn't think I should stand up. "Why do you push us around?" I asked him. And he said, "I don't know. But the law is the law and you are under arrest." As soon as he said that I stood up, [and] the three of us left the bus together.…

❝[The bus driver] said I should stand up, and I said, 'No, I will not.'❞

Rosa Parks was fingerprinted after being arrested for not giving up her bus seat to a white man. ▶

INTEGRATION

Under the leadership of Dr. Martin Luther King Jr., who was becoming an important civil rights leader, blacks in Montgomery started a bus boycott and stopped riding the busses. On the first day of the boycott, more than forty thousand blacks walked, taxied, cycled, and even hitchhiked their way around town. The boycott was a complete success, and community leaders decided to continue it. The protest lasted until November 1956, when the Supreme Court ruled that segregation of public transportation was unconstitutional.

In September 1957, nine black students were scheduled to enroll in the all-white Central High School in Little Rock, Arkansas, because of a federal court order to integrate. Governor Orval Faubus sent President Eisenhower a telegram asking him to void the order and let Little Rock settle this "local" issue itself.

In response, Eisenhower sent Faubus a reply in which he explained

FAUBUS'S TELEGRAM TO PRESIDENT EISENHOWER: 1957

Mr. President:

... The question in issue at Little Rock at this moment is not integration vs. segregation....

The question now is whether or not the head of a sovereign state can exercise his constitutional powers and discretion....

I appeal to you to use your good offices to modify the extreme stand and stop the unwarranted interference of federal agents ... so that we may again enjoy domestic tranquility and continue in our pursuit of ideal relations between the races.

... May I have the assurance of your understanding and cooperation?

▲ President Eisenhower *(left)* and Governor Faubus in 1957.

that he, Eisenhower, was president of all the people, and that he had a responsibility to make sure that federal court orders were enforced.

Congress—often slow to act on issues—could no longer ignore recent Supreme Court decisions and the

EISENHOWER'S TELEGRAM TO FAUBUS: 1957

... When I became President, I took an oath to support and defend the Constitution of the United States. The only assurance I can give you is that the Federal Constitution will be upheld by me by every legal means at my command....

0

activism of black Americans. With the backing of Lyndon Johnson, the Senate majority leader, Congress passed the first civil rights legislation since Reconstruction. The Civil Rights Act of 1957 created the Commission on Civil Rights to investigate cases in which the right to vote was denied on the basis of either race or a violation of the equal protection clauses of the Fourteenth Amendment.

On September 23, when the black students tried to attend classes at Little Rock Central High School, an angry mob surrounded the school, and the students were forced to leave. As a result, President Eisenhower ordered U.S. Army troops and the Arkansas National Guard to protect the students and make sure they were allowed to go to school.

◄ African American students arrive at Little Rock Central High School under federal protection in October 1957.

CHAPTER 3

The Kennedy Years

1960–1963

In 1960, the Republicans chose Vice President Richard M. Nixon to run against John F. Kennedy, the Democratic candidate. Most people believed that the two candidates were evenly matched, but the turning point was a series of television debates. Kennedy looked younger and more in control. Nixon looked unsavory and came across as heavy-jowled and surly. More than half of all voters reported that the debates influenced their opinions of the candidates. Kennedy won the election by a razor-thin margin of 119,450 votes.

The "Great Debates" had a significant impact beyond the election of 1960, as well. They created a precedent in American presidential politics. Federal laws were passed requiring that all candidates receive equal airtime. Debates between candidates, in one form or another, have become a fixture of U.S. presidential politics.

CAMELOT

John F. Kennedy was the youngest person ever elected president of the United States. From the very first day of his administration, he was surrounded by an aura of idealism and even glamour. Never before had so many Americans related to a president and his family. They saw in the Kennedys the greatness of the American Dream.

In just three generations, the Kennedys had gone from being poor Irish immigrants to being a rich, large family that dominated the White House and the American political

▲ Presidential debates were televised for the first time in 1960.

scene. The Kennedys were perceived by many as a royal family, who lived in their private "Camelot."

President Kennedy said that the 1960s presented a New Frontier, and he challenged Americans to be pioneers. He gave many people a renewed sense of purpose and inspired them to contribute their talents to society.

▲ Some admirers of the Kennedy family saw them as if they were royalty.

KENNEDY'S INAUGURAL ADDRESS: 1961

... Since this country was founded, each generation of Americans has been summoned to give testimony to its national loyalty. The graves of young Americans who answered the call to service surround the globe.

Now the trumpet summons us again—not as a call to bear arms, though arms we need; not as a call to battle, though embattled we are—but a call to bear the burden of a long twilight struggle, year in and year out, "rejoicing in hope, patient in tribulation," a struggle against the common enemies of man: tyranny, poverty, disease, and war itself.

Can we forge against these enemies a grand and global alliance, north and south, east and west, that can assure a more fruitful life for all mankind? Will you join in that historic effort?...

And so, my fellow Americans: Ask not what your country can do for you—ask what you can do for your country.

My fellow citizens of the world: Ask not what America will do for you, but what together we can do for the freedom of man....

❝ Ask not what your country can do for you—ask what you can do for your country. **❞**

THE START OF THE SPACE RACE

On April 12, 1961, the Soviet Union announced that one of its cosmonauts (astronauts), Yuri A. Gagarin, had made the world's first orbital flight. President Kennedy was dismayed that the United States was second to the Soviets in the space race. He called on Vice President Lyndon Johnson, the chairman of the National Space Council, to determine what national space program project promised dramatic results and would show America's supremacy in space.

On May 8, Johnson's survey recommended space flights with human beings. As for the best way to put the nation ahead of the Soviets, the report suggested a manned lunar landing. "It is man, not mere machines, in space that captures the imagination of the world," the report said. Such a project would recover the nation's loss of prestige and stimulate advances in space technology.

On May 25, President Kennedy announced that the United States

KENNEDY'S MEMO TO VICE PRESIDENT JOHNSON: 1961

In accordance with our conversation I would like for you as Chairman of the Space Council to be in charge of making an overall survey of where we stand in space.

1. Do we have a chance of beating the Soviets by putting a laboratory in space, or by a trip around the moon, or by a rocket to land on the moon, or by a rocket to go to the moon and back with a man? Is there any other space program which promises dramatic results in which we could win?

2. How much additional would it cost?

3. Are we working 24 hours a day on existing programs? If not, why not? If not, will you make recommendations to me as to how work can be speeded up.

4. In building large boosters should we put our emphasis on nuclear, chemical or liquid fuel, or a combination of these three?

5. Are we making maximum effort? Are we achieving necessary results?

... I would appreciate a report on this at the earliest possible moment.

intended to land an American on the moon and return him safely to earth before the end of the decade.

BAY OF PIGS

In 1959, Cuban revolutionary Fidel Castro led a coup in Cuba and deposed dictator Fulgencio Batista, whom the U.S. government supported. In January 1961, President Eisenhower broke off

▲ Just before the Bay of Pigs invasion in 1961, Cuban recruits get a physical exam in Miami, Florida.

diplomatic relations with Castro's Cuba. But the CIA was already training Cuban exiles—some of whom were American residents—for a possible invasion of the island.

When John F. Kennedy became president, he approved a plan to create an invasion force that would land at two beaches on the southern coast of Cuba at the Bay of Pigs in order to overthrow the Communist government of Castro. Some of the members of Kennedy's cabinet fully supported the secret operation, while others were anxious about it. Arthur Schlesinger, one of the president's aides, urged the president in a memo to think about damage control measures if the operation was revealed.

On April 17, fifteen hundred Cuban exiles armed with American weapons landed at the Bay of Pigs, but during the first few hours of the operation, it became quite clear that the exiles would likely lose the battle. President Kennedy was unwilling to commit any American ground troops to help overthrow Castro and instead chose to abandon both the operation and the Cuban exiles. By the time the fighting ended on April 19, ninety Cuban exiles were dead and the rest had been taken prisoner. The failure of the invasion severely embarrassed President Kennedy and the United States. Castro, wary of possible future American incursions into Cuba, sought closer relations with the Soviet Union.

SCHLESINGER'S MEMO TO KENNEDY: 1961

... A great many people simply do not at this moment see that Cuba presents so grave and compelling a threat to our national security as to justify a course of which much of the world will interpret as calculated aggression against a small nation....

When lies must be told, they should be told by subordinate officials. At no point should the President be asked to lend himself to the cover operation. For this reason ... someone other than the President should make the final decision [to invade Cuba] and do so in his absence—someone whose head can later be placed in the block if things go terribly wrong....

> **"When lies must be told, they should be told by subordinate officials."**

THE CUBAN MISSILE CRISIS

In 1962, the U.S. government learned that the Soviet Union had secretly installed nuclear weapons in Cuba in order to shift the nuclear balance of power away from the United States. This move may have been a reaction to placement of U.S. missiles in Turkey, not far from the Soviet border. Because Cuba is only ninety miles from Florida, the Soviets saw putting missiles there as a quick way to threaten the United States.

In late July 1962, President Kennedy was told that more than sixty Soviet ships were en route to Cuba and that they were probably carrying missiles. Photographs from American spy planes confirmed the

▲ **President Kennedy and Premier Khrushchev greet each other in Vienna, Austria, in 1961.**

construction of missile sites near San Cristobal. On October 22, President Kennedy sent a letter to Khrushchev

KENNEDY'S LETTER TO KHRUSHCHEV: 1962

Sir:

... At our meeting in Vienna and subsequently, I expressed our readiness and desire to find, through peaceful negotiation, a solution to any and all problems that divide us. At the same time ... the United States could not tolerate any action on your part which in a major way disturbed the existing over-all balance of the power in the world....

I publicly stated that if certain developments in Cuba took place, the United States would do whatever must be done to protect its own security and that of its allies.

Despite this, the rapid development of long-range missile bases and other offensive weapons systems in Cuba has proceeded. I must tell you that the United States is determined that this threat to the security of this hemisphere be removed.... The action we are taking [a naval blockade of Soviet ships headed to Cuba] is the minimum necessary to remove the threat to the security of the nations of this hemisphere....

I hope that your Government will refrain from any action which would widen ... this already grave crisis and that we can ... resume the path of peaceful negotiation.

telling him that the United States would do whatever was necessary to protect its own security and that of its allies. In a television address, President Kennedy announced that any nuclear missile attack from Cuba would be regarded as an attack by the Soviet Union and would be responded to accordingly. He also announced a naval quarantine of Cuba to prevent further Soviet shipments of military weapons.

The entire world was terrified that a nuclear war was imminent. After several tense days, Khrushchev offered to dismantle the missile bases, if the United States would pledge not to invade Cuba. In secret, the U.S. also agreed to remove its missiles in Turkey. Khrushchev ordered the removal of all Soviet missiles in Cuba. Satisfied, President Kennedy ordered an end to the quarantine of Cuba on November 20.

1963 CIVIL RIGHTS MARCH

By 1963, black Americans were pushing the civil rights movement in new directions.

In June, Kennedy proposed legislation that would prohibit a number of discriminatory practices and would increase the authority of the civil rights division of the Department of Justice to deal with the issues, but a number of Southern senators and congressmen moved to block the measure. On August 28, while Congress was debating the bill, black civil rights activists staged the "March on Washington for Jobs and Freedom." More than two hundred fifty thousand people—including sixty thousand whites—marched from the Washington Monument to the Lincoln Memorial. It was the largest demonstration ever to take place in the nation's capital. The marchers listened to prominent black and white leaders, but the highlight of the event was a speech by Dr. Martin Luther King Jr. in which he revealed his dream for a color-blind United States.

▲ African Americans march on Washington, D.C., in 1963.

KING'S "I HAVE A DREAM" SPEECH: 1963

... I say to you today, my friends, that in spite of the difficulties and frustrations of the moment, I still have a dream ... that one day this nation will rise up and live out the true meaning of its creed: "We hold these truths to be self-evident: that all men are created equal."

I have a dream that one day ... the sons of former slaves and the sons of former slaveowners will be able to sit down together at a table of brotherhood....

I have a dream that my four little children will one day live in a nation where they will not be judged by the color of their skin but by the content of their character. I have a dream today!

I have a dream that one day [in] the state of Alabama ... little black boys and black girls will be able to join hands with little white boys and white girls as sisters and brothers. I have a dream today....

This is our hope. This is the faith with which I return to the South....

With this faith we will be able to work together, to pray together, to struggle together, to go to jail together, to stand up for freedom together, knowing that we will be free one day....

When we let freedom ring ... [we] will be able to join hands and sing ... "Free at last, free at last; thank God Almighty, we are free at last."

KENNEDY IS ASSASSINATED

On November 22, 1963, President Kennedy was assassinated in Dallas, Texas, while riding in a motorcade. Lee Harvey Oswald, a former Marine with ties to both Cuba and the Soviet Union, was accused of the murder. A few days after Oswald's arrest, he was shot by Jack Ruby, a Dallas nightclub owner, who had been a great admirer of President Kennedy.

Vice President Lyndon B. Johnson took over the presidency and later appointed a commission to investigate President Kennedy's assassination. It was headed by the chief justice of the Supreme Court, Earl Warren. Its final report, issued in September 1964, concluded that Oswald had killed Kennedy and that he had acted alone. However, some felt the report left many questions unanswered, and it did not put to rest the theory that the assassination was part of a much larger conspiracy.

▲ Cameras caught the shooting of Lee Harvey Oswald by Jack Ruby in 1963.

CHAPTER 4

Johnson's Great Society

1963 – 1969

In the months following President Kennedy's assassination, President Johnson persuaded Congress to enact a wide range of programs that would help the United States achieve his vision of a "Great Society"—one in which poverty, disease, and racial injustice were eliminated.

Growing up poor in Texas, Johnson knew what poverty meant. Early in 1964, he declared a "war on poverty" through the Economic Opportunity Act. It provided funds for the Job Corps, an organization that provided employment for inner-city youths, and Head Start, an education program for disadvantaged preschoolers.

During the Democratic Convention in August 1964, the delegates wanted President Johnson as their party's candidate, but Johnson didn't know if he would accept the nomination or not, because he believed the American people didn't support him. His success in handling domestic problems had been overshadowed by the deepening crisis in Vietnam. He told his press secretary, George Reedy, "I have a desire to unite the people, and the South is against me, and the North is against me, and the Negroes are against me, and the press doesn't really have an affection for me."

It took a letter from Johnson's wife, Lady Bird, to convince him he was wrong and that he should finish the job that she felt he was born to do. On election day, Johnson won a landslide victory over Barry Goldwater, the conservative Republican candidate.

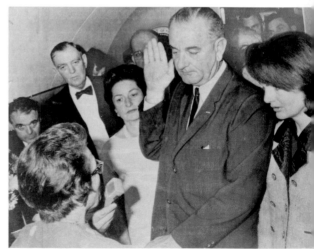

▲ Vice President Johnson took the presidential oath of office on Air Force One.

Beloved—

You are as brave a man as Harry Truman—or FDR—or Lincoln. You can go on to find some peace, some achievement amidst all the pain. You have been strong, patient, determined beyond any words of mine to express.

I honor you for it. So does most of the country.

To step out now would be wrong for your country, and I can see nothing but a lonely waste land for your future. Your friends would be frozen in embarrassed silence and your enemies jeering.

I am not afraid of Time [magazine, which had recently written an article critical of the first lady] or lies or losing money or defeat.

In the final analysis I can't carry any of the burdens you talked of—so I know it's only your choice. But I know you are as brave as any of the thirty-five [other presidents of the United States].

I love you always.

Bird

PRESIDENT JOHNSON AND CIVIL RIGHTS

President Johnson's Great Society programs also addressed the issues of racial injustice in the United States. The Civil Rights Act of 1964 ended segregation in public accommodations, authorized the United States attorney general to file lawsuits to integrate public schools that were still segregated, and created the Equal Employment Opportunity Commission that would investigate any complaints of discrimination in the workplace.

▲ An undated photograph of Lady Bird Johnson taken behind the White House.

CIVIL RIGHTS ACT: 1964

… No person … shall, in determining whether any individual is qualified … to vote in any Federal election, apply any standard, practice, or procedure different from the standards, practices, or procedures applied under such law or laws to other individuals within the same county, parish, or similar political subdivision who have been found by State officials to be qualified to vote.…

All persons shall be entitled to the full and equal enjoyment of the goods, services, facilities, and privileges, advantages, and accommodations of any place of public accommodation … without discrimination or segregation on the ground of race, color, religion, or national origin.…

It shall be an unlawful … practice for an employer to fail or refuse to hire or to discharge any individual, or otherwise to discriminate against any individual with respect to his compensation, terms, conditions, or privileges of employment, because of such individual's race, color, religion, sex, or national origin.…

In the summer of 1964, the Congress of Racial Equality (CORE) and the Student Nonviolent Coordinating Committee (SNCC) organized the Mississippi Summer Project. Its goal was to register as many black voters in that state as possible. In March 1965, Martin Luther King Jr. decided to lead a march from Selma to Montgomery, Alabama, in order to draw attention to the inequities in voter registration. King chose Selma because out of its fifteen thousand black residents, only three hundred fifty-five were registered to vote.

During the march, the Selma sheriff and his deputies used whips, clubs, and tear gas against the peaceful demonstrators. It was the first time that many Americans had witnessed such brutal force to deny people their legal rights.

African Americans now wanted more than just integration—they wanted racial equality. The Voting Rights Act of 1965 did away with literacy tests, provided for federal examiners to register voters, and gave the United States attorney general the authority to begin lawsuits against states that still charged a poll tax (a prerequisite tax for voting). In 1966, the Supreme Court ruled that the poll

tax was illegal in all state and local elections.

All these legal changes dramatically increased the number of black voters in the South, from approximately one million in 1964 to more than three million by 1968. These voters changed the political landscape of the South. African Americans now formed an important voting bloc in all elections.

◀ Martin Luther King Jr. lead other African Americans in the Selma-Montgomery March in 1965.

TWENTY-FOURTH AMENDMENT: 1964

… The right of citizens of the United States to vote in any primary or other election for President or Vice President, or for Senator or Representative in Congress, shall not be denied or abridged by the United States or any State by reason of failure to pay any poll tax or other tax.…

VOTING RIGHTS ACT: 1965

… No citizen shall be denied the right to vote … because of his failure to comply with any test [to] demonstrate the ability to read, write, understand, or interpret any matter.…

Congress declares [unconstitutional] the requirement of … a poll tax.…

RACE RIOTS

During the 1960s there were outbreaks of violence in many black urban neighborhoods. Many African Americans, especially some in the North, started to believe that the nonviolent civil rights movement of

Martin Luther King Jr. would not gain them full equal rights. Some, like activist Malcolm X, who was assassinated in 1965, thought that violence was justified and that blacks needed power, not white friendship. Many blacks decided to turn his thoughts into deeds. They fought with police in the Watts section of Los Angeles. Anger over their joblessness and what they saw as a lack of opportunity to better themselves sparked the riots. In the end, twenty-eight blacks died.

Other American cities also witnessed serious rioting. In July 1967, twenty-three people were killed in street battles between blacks and police in Newark, New Jersey. In Detroit, a race riot led to the deaths of forty-three people. Ray Rogers of the *New York Post* interviewed a young black man who had participated in the riot.

> **66'Man, they killed Malcolm X just like that. So I'm gonna take a few of them with me.'99**

ROGERS'S ACCOUNT OF THE DETROIT RACE RIOT: 1967

…"We had them—cops so scared that first night they were shooting at one another. I know I got one or two of them, but I don't think I killed them. I wish I had.…"

The young man explained that he went and got his "piece" [gun] after he and his buddy had looted a liquor store.

"We drank a little. And after a while—boom, just like that we deiced to do some shootin."…

Did he realize he could be killed?

"I'm not crazy—I'm not crazy to be killed. I'm just gettin' even for what they did to us. Really. That's where it's at."

"Man, they killed Malcolm X just like that. So I'm gonna take a few of them with me.…"

He explained that he avoided the area patrolled by the airborne troops because of the intensity with which they returned fire.

"They got a lot of soul brothers in their outfit too and I'm not trying to waste my own kind. I am after them honkies.…"

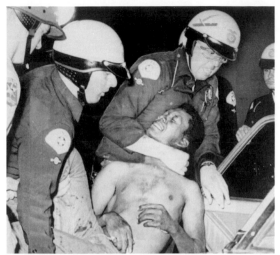

▲ Police subdue a black rioter in the Watts section of Los Angeles in 1965.

RISE OF FEMINISM

In 1963, author Betty Friedan wrote in *The Feminine Mystique* that women should be allowed to find their own identity and not be limited to roles of wife and mother. It was considered the beginning of the feminist movement in the United States. Now women wanted the same rights as men: to own companies, to serve in the military, to hold high political office—to name just a few. In 1966, the National Organization for Women (NOW) was founded. It addressed such issues as helping working mothers by giving federal aid to day-care centers, guaranteeing women the right to an abortion, eliminating job discrimination based on gender, and ensuring equal pay for equal work.

NOW STATEMENT OF PURPOSE: 1966

… We, men and women who hereby constitute ourselves as the National Organization for Women, believe that the time has come for … true equality for all women in America, and … full equal partnership of the sexes, as part of the world-wide revolution of human rights now taking place.…

The purpose of NOW is to take action to bring women into full participation in the mainstream of American society now, exercising all the privileges and responsibilities thereof in truly equal partnership with men.…

We believe that … the protection guaranteed by the U.S. Constitution to the civil rights of all individuals, must be effectively applied and enforced to isolate and remove patterns of sex discrimination, to ensure equality of opportunity in employment and education, and equality of civil and political rights and responsibilities on behalf of women, as well as for Negroes and other deprived groups.…

START OF THE VIETNAM CONFLICT

A foreign policy of supporting the non-Communist leaders of South Vietnam had been established by the Eisenhower administration, when Vietnam was divided into Communist and non-Communist parts in 1954. Presidents Kennedy and Johnson continued this support during their terms.

In August 1964, North Vietnamese patrol boats fired on American destroyers in the Gulf of Tonkin. Congress passed a resolution that gave President Johnson authority to use military force in Southeast Asia. In early 1965, President Johnson ordered the bombing of North Vietnam. The first American combat troops arrived in South Vietnam in March 1965.

▲ U.S. aircraft lined up in Da Nang, South Vietnam, in September 1965.

THE GULF OF TONKIN RESOLUTION: 1964

... Whereas naval units of the Communist regime in Vietnam, in violation of the principles of the Charter of the United Nations and of international law, have deliberately and repeatedly attacked the United States naval vessels ... and have thereby created a serious threat to international peace;...

Whereas the United States is assisting the people of southeast Asia to protect their political freedom and has no territorial, military or political ambitions in that area:... Now, therefore be it

Resolved ... that the Congress approves ... the determination of the President, as Commander in Chief, to take all necessary measures to repel any armed attack against ... the United States and to prevent further aggression....

PROTESTS AT HOME

Within weeks, antiwar protests broke out on college campuses. Students held rallies and marches. During the next two years, the antiwar movement increased with numerous peace marches held around the country.

At that time, many young men were drafted—or called into service— by the military. Some of them who did not believe in the war burned their draft cards in protest. Even GIs stationed overseas began supporting the antiwar movement in whatever ways they could, from wearing peace symbols to refusing to obey orders.

Activists, celebrities, and musicians such as Abbie Hoffman, Timothy Leary, Allen Ginsberg, Jane Fonda, Jimi Hendrix, Jefferson Airplane, Joan Baez, and Bob Dylan and countless others took up the antiwar cause. Many of them made speeches and music that reflected the anger that Americans felt over the Vietnam War—especially as more young GIs came home in body bags.

Although written before the Vietnam War, Pete Seeger's "Where Have All the Flowers Gone" spoke of the futility of war and the need for peace in the world. It was revived and made popular in 1962 by the trio Peter, Paul, and Mary.

▲ In 1965, students from the University of Texas protest the Vietnam War.

"WHERE HAVE ALL THE FLOWER'S GONE": 1956

Where have all the soldiers gone?
Long time passing
Where have all the soldiers gone?
Long time ago
Where have all the soldiers gone?
Gone to graveyards every one
When will they ever learn!
When will they ever learn!

JOHNSON AND VIETNAM

On January 30, 1968, the North Vietnamese Army and the Viet Cong launched the Tet Offensive—a month-long attack against more than one hundred cities and military bases in South Vietnam. Although the campaign proved to be a military disaster for the Communists because of the heavy loss of life and equipment, it had a great psychological impact in the United States. Many Americans now felt that the war could not be won without a major escalation in which more powerful (perhaps even nuclear) weapons would be used.

In the wake of the Tet Offensive, President Johnson's popularity plummeted. Senator Eugene McCarthy of Minnesota had just made a surprisingly strong showing in the New Hampshire Democratic presidential primary, and Senator Robert F. Kennedy had also decided to enter the presidential race. On March 31, President Johnson announced to the American people that the bombing of much of North Vietnam would stop and that he would neither seek nor accept the Democratic party's nomination for president.

▲ U.S. troops in Vietnam rescue a fellow soldier under hostile fire.

JOHNSON'S BROADCAST ADDRESS: MARCH 31, 1968

Good evening, my fellow Americans. Tonight I want to speak to you of peace in Vietnam and Southeast Asia....

Tonight, I renew that offer I made last August—to stop the bombardment of North Vietnam. We ask that talks begin promptly, that they be serious talks on the substance of peace. We assume that during those talks Hanoi will not take advantage of our restraint.

We are prepared to move immediately toward peace through negotiations. So, tonight, in the hope that this action will lead to early talks, I am taking the first step to de-escalate the conflict. We are reducing ... the present level of hostilities. And we are doing so unilaterally, and at once.

Tonight, I have ordered our aircraft and our naval vessels to make no attacks on North Vietnam, except in the area north of the Demilitarized Zone where the continuing enemy buildup directly threatens allied forward positions and where the movement of their troops and supplies are clearly related to that threat....

It is our fervent hope that North Vietnam ... will now cease its efforts to achieve a military victory and will join with us in moving toward the peace table....

There is division in the American house now.... And holding the trust that is mine, as president of all the people, I cannot disregard the peril to the progress of the American people and the hope and the prospect of peace for all peoples....

I have concluded that I should not permit the presidency to become involved in the partisan divisions that are developing in this political year....

Accordingly, I shall not seek, and I will not accept, the nomination of my party for another term as your president....

> **66** Accordingly, I shall not seek, and I will not accept, the nomination of my party for another term as your president. **99**

1968—A Year of Violence and Killing

After Johnson's speech, the main contenders for the Democratic nomination were Vice President Hubert Humphrey, who defended the administration's policies in Vietnam, and Senator Robert Kennedy of New York, who argued against Johnson's policies.

On June 5, 1968, Senator Kennedy was shot by Sirhan Sirhan, an Arab-American who was infuriated by the senator's strong pro-Israel positions. Senator Kennedy died the next day, and Vice President Humphrey won the party's nomination at the violence-marred Democratic convention in Chicago in August. While the convention was taking place, bloody battles erupted on the streets between antiwar and civil rights demonstrators and the police. Later that year, former Vice President Richard M. Nixon won the presidential election.

On April 4, just a few months before Kennedy's assassination, Martin Luther King Jr. had been assassinated in Memphis, Tennessee, by James Earl Ray, an avowed racist. King's death deepened the sense of bitterness and hostility among African Americans, both moderate and militant, and led to rioting in several U.S. cities, including Wash-ington. Ironically, just before his own assassination, Robert Kennedy had delivered a speech in Indianapolis, Indiana, on the death of Reverend King.

Pop Culture of the 1960s

The decade of the 1960s was a time when long-held values and norms of behavior broke down. In the early 60s, some young people thought it was daring just to listen to the music of the Beatles, a rock group from Great Britain. By the late 60s, some young people simply "dropped out" and separated themselves from mainstream culture. They were called "hippies," and were often sexually promiscuous and used recreational drugs, such as marijuana and hallucinogenic LSD. Their "counterculture" was reflected in the rock music of the time by such performers as Jim Morrison and Janis Joplin.

A major counterculture event occurred in upstate New York in August 1969. The Woodstock Festival was billed as "three days of peace, music, and love," and almost four hundred thousand people attended this overwhelming event. On August 17, Bernard L. Collier described the festival in an article in the *New York Times*.

COLLIER'S ACCOUNT OF THE WOODSTOCK FESTIVAL: 1969

… Waves of weary youngsters streamed away from the Woodstock Music and Art Fair last night and early today as security officials reported at least two deaths and 4,000 people treated for injuries, illness and adverse drug reactions over the festival's three-day period.…

Young people straggling into the Port of New York Authority bus terminal at 41st Street and Eighth Avenue last night were damp, disheveled and given to such wild eccentricities of dress as the wearing of a battered top hat with grimy jersey, blue jeans and sandals. They were, according to a driver, Richard Biccum, "good kids in disguise." Mr. Biccum … said, "I'll haul kids any day rather than commuters, because they were exceptionally polite and orderly."…

THE MOON LANDING

In 1961, when President Kennedy said that the United States would put a man on the moon and bring him back safely to Earth by the end of the decade, many Americans thought this sounded like science fiction. But the idea gave a great boost to the American people's spirits, because in the previous four years they had watched the Soviet Union take the lead in the space race. On July 20, 1969, after a four-day trip, *Apollo* astronauts Neil Armstrong and Edwin "Buzz" Aldrin landed on the moon. When Neil Armstrong left the lunar module and stepped on the

▲ Neil Armstrong plants the U.S. flag on the surface of the moon in 1969.

moon's surface, more than a half billion people around the world heard him say, "That's one small step for man, one giant leap for mankind."

TIME LINE

1950	■ Korean War begins when North Korea invades South Korea.
1950–1954	■ Senator Joseph R. McCarthy accuses many public figures of being Communists.
1952	■ Dwight D. Eisenhower is elected the thirty-fourth U.S. president.
1952	■ Dr. Jonas Salk discovers a vaccine for polio.
1953	■ Julius and Ethel Rosenberg are executed for espionage.
1953	■ Armistice is signed ending Korean War.
1955	■ Rosa Parks refuses to give up her bus seat to a white man; this eventually leads to desegregation in public transportation.
1957	■ President Eisenhower sends federal troops to Little Rock, Arkansas, to enforce school integration.
1960	■ John F. Kennedy is elected the thirty-fifth U.S. president.
1961	■ The Soviet Union sends the first man into space.
1961	■ The United States invasion of Cuba fails.
1962	■ The Cuban Missile Crisis almost causes nuclear war.
1963	■ Blacks and whites protest peacefully in Washington, D.C.
1963	■ President Kennedy is assassinated in Dallas, Texas; Vice President Lyndon Johnson becomes the thirty-sixth U.S. president.
1964	■ President Johnson signs the Civil Rights Act.
1965	■ President Johnson orders the bombing of North Vietnam; U.S. troops arrive in South Vietnam.
1965	■ President Johnson signs the Voting Rights Act.
1968	■ North Vietnam launches the Tet Offensive.
1968	■ Reverend Martin Luther King, Jr., and Senator Robert F. Kennedy are assassinated a few months apart.
1968	■ Richard M. Nixon is elected the thirty-seventh U.S. president.
1969	■ U.S. astronauts Armstrong and Aldrin land on the moon.

GLOSSARY

armistice: end of hostilities in a war.

astronauts: people trained to fly in space.

Camelot: legendary town where King Arthur had his court; nickname for President Kennedy's administration.

CIA: Central Intelligence Agency—government organization that spies for the United States.

civil rights: rights guaranteed to individuals because they are citizens of the United States.

clemency: kindness or mercy shown toward an offender.

Cold War: non-military struggle mostly between the United States and the Soviet Union for world domination between 1945 and 1991.

counterculture: the culture of some young people that is contrary to that of their parents.

demagogue: a person who distorts facts to stir up people.

demilitarized zone: an area where military battles can't be fought.

feminism: a belief that women should have the same rights as men.

Free World: countries that have democratic forms of government

hippies: persons of the 1960s who reject conventional society and live a free-spirited life.

inner city: crowded, low-income, older part of a city.

McCarthyism: a movement in the 1950s when people were accused of being disloyal to their government without sufficient evidence to prove it.

NAACP: National Association for the Advancement of Colored People—an organization promoting equal rights for blacks.

naval quarantine: an order to keep ships from entering another country's ports.

NOW: National Organization for Women—a group promoting equal rights for women.

parallel: an imaginary east-west line that encircles the earth.

placate: to keep someone from getting angry about something.

polio: a disease that affects the muscles.

poll tax: money that people have to pay in order to vote; it was a way to keep blacks from voting.

pop culture: popular forms of entertainment.

public works: government projects meant to create jobs for people.

subversion: an attempt to ruin or destroy something, usually a government.

subversives: people who try to overthrow a government.

Tet Offensive: Vietnam War battle that took place during the Vietnamese New Year holidays.

FURTHER INFORMATION

BOOKS

Buhle, Paul, and David Wagner. *Hide in Plain Sight: The Hollywood Blacklistees in Film and Television, 1950–2000*. Palgrave Macmillan, 2003.

Stanley, George E. *Harry S. Truman: Thirty-Third President of the United States,* Childhood of Famous Americans. Simon & Schuster/Aladdin Books, 2004.

Turck, Mary. *The Civil Rights Movement for Kids: A History with 21 Activities*. Chicago Review Press, 2000.

WEB SITES

www.cnn.com/SPECIALS/cold.war/ This Web site by CNN (Cable News Network) explores the Cold War experience from the point of view of culture, technology, espionage, and the bomb.

www.cr.nps.gov/nr/travel/civilrights/index.htm This Web site titled "We Shall Overcome" is sponsored by the National Park Service and explores the historic places associated with the civil rights movement.

USEFUL ADDRESSES

National Civil Rights Museum
450 Mulberry Street
Memphis, TN 38103
Telephone: (901) 521-9699

Smithsonian National Air and Space Museum
6th and Independence Avenue, SW
Washington, DC 20560
Telephone: (202) 357-2700

★★★ INDEX ★★★